The Role of International Law in light of the COVID-19 Global Pandemic

Brian Khisa

Bibliographic information published by the German National Library:

The German National Library lists this publication in the National Bibliography; detailed bibliographic data are available on the Internet at http://dnb.dnb.de.

ISBN: 9783346972972
This book is also available as an ebook.

© GRIN Publishing GmbH
Trappentreustraße 1
80339 München

Print and binding: Books on Demand GmbH, Norderstedt, Germany
Printed on acid-free paper from responsible sources.

The present work has been carefully prepared. Nevertheless, authors and publishers do not incur liability for the correctness of information, notes, links and advice as well as any printing errors.

GRIN web shop: https://www.grin.com/document/1418814

The Role of International Law in light of the COVID-19 Global Pandemic

BRIAN KHISA SIMIYU

MENTAL WEALTH - INTERNATIONAL LAW: PROBLEMS AND PROCESS

JANUARY 25, 2021

ABSTRACT

In light of the COVID-19 pandemic, this research seeks to analyse the impact of the global health crisis on the international legal order. The main argument is that while the focus of international law has been on the elimination of war towards global peace and security, the COVID-19 pandemic has shed light on the shortcomings of international law in dealing with a global health crisis. By considering the specialized mechanisms under international law for dealing with a pandemic, the research will reveal the critical role that international law can play in fostering global health. The research is based on a qualitative examination utilizing a deliberate audit of extensive literature on international law and the COVID-19 pandemic. Secondary data obtained from relevant journal articles, textbooks, reports and internet sources.

TABLE OF CONTENTS

1.0   INTRODUCTION

The year 2020 has been that year we all wish we could remember to forget. On the one hand, it was the year that marked the beginning of a new decade, which was greeted with optimism and hope for a brighter future. On the other hand, and perhaps fatefully, it turned out to be the year when our human existence hung on the balance with the emergence of an invisible and relentless enemy. Just as the world prepared to usher in the new year on 31st December 2019, reports emanating from China revealed the eruption of a novel coronavirus based on several cases of unusual pneumonia detected in the City of Wuhan, Hubei Province.[1]

The gravity of the novel coronavirus outbreak would, later on, become apparent with far-reaching global implications. This followed with a declaration by the World Health Organization of the novel coronavirus as a 'public health emergency of international concern' on 30th January 2020[2] and the designation of the virus as severe acute respiratory syndrome coronavirus (SARS-CoV-2) and the disease it causes as the coronavirus disease (COVID-19).[3] Consequently, COVID-19 was declared by the WHO to be a global pandemic on 11th March 2020.[4] The current COVID-19 global situation according to the World Health Organization as at the date of this writing stands at 96,877,399 confirmed cases and 2,098,879 reported deaths.[5]

---

[1] WHO, 'Listings of WHO's Response to COVID-19' (*www.who.int*, 2020) <https://www.who.int/news/item/29-06-2020-covidtimeline> accessed 31 December 2020.

[2] 'IHR Emergency Committee on Novel Coronavirus (2019-NCoV)' (*www.who.int*) <https://www.who.int/director-general/speeches/detail/who-director-general-s-statement-on-ihr-emergency-committee-on-novel-coronavirus-(2019-ncov)> accessed 31 December 2020.

[3] World Health Organization, 'Naming the Coronavirus Disease (COVID-19) and the Virus That Causes It' (*www.who.int*, 2020) <https://www.who.int/emergencies/diseases/novel-coronavirus-2019/technical-guidance/naming-the-coronavirus-disease-(covid-2019)-and-the-virus-that-causes-it> accessed 31 December 2020.

[4] WHO, 'WHO Director-General's Opening Remarks at the Media Briefing on COVID-19 - 11 March 2020' (*www.who.int*, 2020) <https://www.who.int/director-general/speeches/detail/who-director-general-s-opening-remarks-at-the-media-briefing-on-covid-19---11-march-2020> accessed 31 December 2020.

[5] World Health Organization, 'WHO COVID-19 Dashboard' (*covid19.who.int*, 2020) <https://covid19.who.int/> accessed 31 December 2020.

In light of the COVID-19 pandemic, this research seeks to analyse the impact of the global health crisis on the international legal order. The main argument advanced is that while the focus of international law has been on the elimination of war towards global peace and security, the COVID-19 pandemic has shed light on the shortcomings of international law in dealing with a global health crisis. By considering the specialized mechanisms under international law for dealing with a pandemic, the research will reveal the critical role that international law can play in fostering global health.

The research begins with a brief historical account of pandemics before narrowing down to the recent COVID-19 pandemic, which delineates the role of international law in the context of a pandemic. The research then shifts focus to the role of the United Nations and the World Health Organization, which bear the ultimate responsibility for a global response to a pandemic. Subsequently, the research ensues with a discussion on the general obligations of states under international law and highlights the key legal and policy responses adopted by states to deal with the COVID-19 pandemic. In conclusion, it is observed and recommended that while states opted to adopt unilateral nationalistic approaches in dealing with the COVID-19 pandemic, the panacea for our mutual survival as humanity lies in the capacity to work as a community in collaboration with each other as that is the fundamental role of international law.

2.0   LITERATURE REVIEW

2.1   Brief Historical Background on Pandemics

The world is no stranger to pandemics. Not many historical events have had a profound impact on humanity such as the outbreak of pandemics.[6] The history of human existence is replete with pandemics that have wreaked havoc while also ironically contributing to technological

---

[66] Damir Huremović, *Psychiatry of Pandemics : A Mental Health Response to Infection Outbreak* (Cham Springer International Publishing Imprint,Springer 2019).

advancement in the field of science, economy and politics.[7] This is well elucidated in Frank Snowden's *Epidemics and Society: From the Black Death to the Present,*[8] where he explores the impact of pandemics and how they have moulded societies uncovering how diseases have affected clinical science and public health, yet additionally transforming arts, religion, intellectual history and warfare.

Perhaps the greatest, if not the worst disease outbreak in mankind's history is the 14th Century epidemic of the bubonic plague,[9] which would, later on, be referred to as The Black Death claiming an estimated 60% of the European population at the time.[10] The Great Influenza Pandemic of 1918[11] could be regarded as the first true global pandemic and the first that happened in the context of contemporary international law. It is estimated to have claimed more lives in one year than the Black Death had killed in a century.[12] In reality, over the last couple of years has been characterized with the emergence of new forms of fast-spreading infectious diseases such as HIV/AIDS, Severe Acute Respiratory Syndrome (SARS), the avian flu or the H1N1, to mention but a few.[13]

2.2   The COVID-19 Global Pandemic

The history of coronavirus dates back to the 1960s with the discovery of infections affecting the human respiratory system, which would, later on, be referred to as coronaviruses because of their crown-like appearance of the surface projections.[14] Later on in the year 2002, an

---

[7] Walter Scheidel, *The Great Leveler : Violence and the History of Inequality from the Stone Age to the Twenty-First Century / Walter Scheidel.* (Princeton University Press 2017).
[8] Frank M Snowden, *Epidemics and Society : From the Black Death to the Present* (Yale University Press 2019).
[9] Ole Benedictow, 'The Black Death: The Greatest Catastrophe Ever | History Today' (*Historytoday.com*, 2005) <https://www.historytoday.com/archive/black-death-greatest-catastrophe-ever> accessed 31 December 2020.
[10] Sharon N DeWitte, 'Mortality Risk and Survival in the Aftermath of the Medieval Black Death' (2014) 9 PLoS ONE <https://www.ncbi.nlm.nih.gov/pmc/articles/PMC4013036/>.
[11] John M Barry, *GREAT INFLUENZA : The Story of the Deadliest Pandemic in History.* (Penguin Books 2020).
[12] Daniel Flecknoe, Benjamin Charles Wakefield and Aidan Simmons, 'Plagues & Wars: The "Spanish Flu" Pandemic as a Lesson from History' (2018) 34 Medicine, Conflict and Survival.
[13] Xavier Pons Rafols, 'International Law and Global Health: An Overview' [2015] Paix et Securite Internationales.
[14] DAJ Tyrrell and others, 'Coronaviridae' (1975) 5 Intervirology.

unknown illness causing severe acute respiratory syndrome (SARS) emanated from southern China in the province of Guangdong and spread to 26 nations infecting more than 8,000 individuals and claiming 774.[15] It would, later on, be established that respiratory symptoms were caused by the SARS coronavirus (SARS-CoV), which exhibited the deficiency in the pre-existing frameworks for observation and reaction to a global pandemic. In mid-2012, a novel Coronavirus, known as Middle East Respiratory Syndrome (MERS) arose in Saudi Arabia introducing as an extreme respiratory ailment, which reignited fears of a pandemic as well as uncovering the shortcomings of international law in dealing with a pandemic.

The COVID-19 disease is an infectious respiratory disease caused by a novel coronavirus, which is structurally related to the SARS virus. The disease had its inceptions in China and has now become a pandemic influencing practically the whole world highlighting the need for global collaboration in dealing with a pandemic. To date, notwithstanding data on the pandemic, numerous countries particularly the top dogs of the United Nations do not have an essential agreement on approaches to viably battle the illness.

2.3   The Role of International Law during a Pandemic

Tracing its origins to the 1648 Treaty of Westphalia, which brought to an end thirty years of war between the Catholic and Protestant factions within the Holy Roman Empire,[16] International Law has been conceptually defined as "a body of principles, customs and rules regulating the behaviour of states in the international system".[17] Hedley Bull further describes an international system as being shaped when at least two states have adequate contact among

---

[15] 'Summary of Probable SARS Cases with Onset of Illness from 1 November 2002 to 31 July 2003' (*www.who.int*)   <https://www.who.int/publications/m/item/summary-of-probable-sars-cases-with-onset-of-illness-from-1-november-2002-to-31-july-2003> accessed 31 December 2020.

[16] Steven Patton, 'The Peace of Westphalia and It Affects on International Relations, Diplomacy and Foreign Policy' (2019) 10 The Histories: <https://digitalcommons.lasalle.edu/the_histories/vol10/iss1/5> accessed 31 December 2020.

[17] James Crawford, *Brownlie's Principles of Public International Law.* (9th edn, Oxford University Press 2019).

them and have an adequate effect on each other's choices to make them act at any rate in some measure-as a component of an entirety.[18]

While analyzing the preparedness of the international community to deal with a pandemic in *Farewell to the God of Plague: Has International Law Prepared Us for the Next Pandemic?*[19] Phelan and Gostin considered the potential sources for the next pandemic and accurately predicted the emergence of novel coronaviruses. In *Public Health Law: Power, Duty, Restraint* Gostin and Wiley further highlighted the effectiveness of the law as a tool of protection for public health.[20] Bull indicates that a global society exists when a gathering of states, aware of certain normal interests and basic qualities, structure a general public as in they imagine themselves to be limited by a typical arrangement of rules in their relations with each other, and offer in the working of basic organizations.[21]

The substance of international law stems from the idea of the states in their international system and the elements of their general relationships. International law is therefore to states wishing to ensure certain interests or accomplish certain objectives, the working of the worldwide framework and the presence of a worldwide society. In the context of the COVID-19 pandemic, international law can play a basic role in forestalling and alleviating the effects of the crisis in two significant ways. First, it builds up the institutional structures and formal cycles through which governments can react to pandemics and sets the limits for the activity of coercive control over people and organizations to alleviate the danger of infection spread.

---

[18] Hedley Bull, *The Anarchical Society : A Study of Order in World Politics* (Columbia University Press 2012).
[19] Alexandra Phelan and Lawrence O Gostin, 'Farewell to the God of Plague: Has International Law Prepared Us for the next Pandemic?' (2014) 15 Georgetown Journal of International Affairs <https://www.jstor.org/stable/43773636> accessed 31 December 2020.
[20] Lawrence O Gostin and Lindsay F Wiley, *Public Health Law : Power, Duty, Restraint* (University Of California Press 2016).
[21] Bull (n 18).

Inside the worldwide framework, international law gives the system to political exchange among States. While this system probably won't ensure agreement on a worldwide issue, it anyway encourages the proceeding with discourse and interest expected to give theoretical clearness in creating legitimate commitments and for States to acquire acknowledgement of such commitments. In respect of pandemics, international law continues to play a fundamental role evidenced by the 19th and 20th-century handling of global pandemics.

2.4   Legal and Institutional Framework on Pandemics

2.4.1   United Nations (UN)

Since its creation in 1945, the United Nations has become the system organization of contemporary worldwide society. Specifically, the constitutive Charter and other legal instruments adopted by the United Nations have shaped the legal framework of contemporary International Law. In particular regard to pandemics, Article 1 of the United Nations Charter declares one of the goals of the United Nations is "to achieve international co-operation in solving international problems of an economic, social, cultural, or humanitarian character".[22]

Accordingly, within the framework of the United Nations is the general mandate to deal with global pandemics. Furthermore, the recognition of peace and security, development and human rights as the pillars of the United Nations system emphasizes the role of international institutions during pandemics.[23] It can therefore be inferred that any danger to global health can also be regarded as a threat to international peace and security from a global and all-encompassing perspective on health.

---

[22] UN Charter
[23] World Summit Outcome of the 2005 World Summit, Resolution 60/1 of the General Assembly, 16 September 2005, par. 9

2.4.2 United Nations Security Council (UNSC)

The Security Council is entrusted with essential duty regarding the upkeep of global harmony and security, described generally as armed conflict and has a wide cluster of instruments available to its in the quest for that order. Notwithstanding this limited mandate, the UN Security Council played a crucial role in dealing with the Ebola outbreak of 2014 by declaring the disease as a threat to international peace and security.[24] Given the worldwide danger to global harmony and security presented by COVID-19, particularly considering the Ebola point of reference, perhaps it can be argued that the Security Council has a role to play in a pandemic.

2.4.3 World Health Organization (WHO)

The World Health Organization (WHO) was established in 1946 as the international authority in health issues.[25] It is empowered under International Law to deal with a global pandemic through the International Health Regulations, 2005.[26] The World Health Organization, as an agency of the United Nations, is the worldwide institution that acts as a command centre on issues of global health. The organization has come under sharp criticism over the years for its apparent inefficiency and ineffectiveness in dealing with a pandemic. In the context of a pandemic, the establishment of a global institution in the name of the World Health Organization is indicative of global health as a mutually shared value amongst states. Accordingly, the Constitution of the World Health Organization[27] and the International Health Regulations[28] signifies those common rules governing the relations among states.

---

[24] UNSC Resolution 2177
[25] Pons Rafols (n 13).
[26] Rebecca Katz and Sarah Kornblet, 'Comparative Analysis of National Legislation in Support of the Revised International Health Regulations: Potential Models for Implementation in the United States' (2010) 100 American Journal of Public Health.
[27] World Health Organization, *Constitution of the World Health Organization.* (The Organization 1989).
[28] World Health Organization, *International Health Regulations (2005).* (World Health Organization 2016).

2.4.4 International Health Regulations (IHR)

The International Health Regulations is a by-product of the International Sanitary Regulations, which was embraced by WHO in 1951 before the subsequent change of name in 1969. The International Health Regulation (IHR) (2005) is a legal framework for international cooperation on public health emergency response. The framework is a binding agreement between 196 countries of the world.

The IHR are a lawfully restricting arrangement of guidelines embraced under the protection of WHO as a worldwide association and are one of the multilateral administrative components carefully zeroing in on worldwide reconnaissance for transmittable infections.[29]

The International Health Regulations aim to provide for a structural framework of harmonized surveillance, reporting, and response across all WHO partner states, with these guidelines binding all member states automatically unless dismissed. The outbreak of SARS in 2002 exposed the inadequacies of international law at the time to deal with a pandemic and this prompted revision of the IHR in 2005 intended to achieve a higher level of global health security.[30] The IHR mandates states to develop their national capacity in the prevention, detection and response to a pandemic.[31]

Accordingly, the IHR (2005) outlines any unusual incident that poses a public health risk to other states through the international spread of disease and potentially requires a coordinated international response to constitute a 'Public Health Emergency of International Concern' (PHEIC).[32] States are thus obligated to inform the WHO of such event within 24 hours of

---

[29] Lawrence O Gostin, 'Global Health Security in an Era of Explosive Pandemic Potential' [2019] SSRN Electronic Journal.Ogibior

[30] Lawrence O Gostin, 'Global Health Security in an Era of Explosive Pandemic Potential' [2019] SSRN Electronic Journal.

[31] Lawrence O Gostin, Roojin Habibi and Benjamin Mason Meier, 'Has Global Health Law Risen to Meet the COVID-19 Challenge? Revisiting the International Health Regulations to Prepare for Future Threats' (2020) 48 The Journal of Law, Medicine & Ethics.

[32] International Health Regulations (IHR) (Geneva: World Health Organization, 2005), art. 1

detection within their boundaries through national IHR focal points.[33] The declaration of PHEIC has since been utilized by WHO multiple times to control the worldwide spread of diseases such as polio, Zika, Influenza H1N1, Ebola (in West Africa and afterwards in the Congo) and most recently, COVID-19.

The IHR further provides for the most extreme public health measures relevant during a pandemic and accommodate rules appropriate to global traffic and travel. These measures cover the basics of health and immunization authorizations for travellers from regions contaminated by an outbreak disease; defatting, sanitizing and disinfecting of boats and aeroplanes and point by point health measures at air terminals and seaports in the domains of WHO Member States. The greatest health measures permitted in outbreak circumstances are applied to secure the country that endures a pandemic against the danger of superfluous monetary and other bans, which could be forced by adjoining neighbours, exchanging accomplices, and different nations.

2.5   Limitations of the Study

This study reflects on the role of international law in the context of the COVID-19 pandemic. In that regard, and given the novelty of the disease, the discussion here is not comprehensive, but instead a starting point in considering the role international law can play during pandemics. The aim of the research is to draw lessons from the applicable experience so far and outline a scope of significant issues while setting forth some possible reactions.

---

[33] Article 6 of the IHR establishes the reporting duty and places an obligation on states to assess events occurring within their territories and timely notify the WHO of all events which may constitute a public health emergency of international concern.

3.0 DISCUSSION

International Law can play an essential role in the control of global pandemics. The emergence of the COVID-19 pandemic has put to test the essential legal foundations of International Law. Philosophical contrasts aggravated international pressures and made disruptiveness in homegrown governmental issues. In this violent setting of force and thoughts, international law has proven to be powerless and deficient to deal with a global pandemic.

3.1 Obligations of States towards the COVID-19 Pandemic

All WHO Member States are obliged to participate in identifying, containing, and controlling general health crises guided by the International Health Regulations. The fundamental obligations of states include the legal obligation to notify WHO of events that may constitute a public health emergency of international concern and the obligation to develop, strengthen and maintain national capacities to detect, assess, notify, report and respond effectively to public health risks and emergencies.

States may utilize an assortment of approaches to control public health hazards and other health matters, including enactment, auxiliary guidelines, announcements and chief requests, just as sets of principles and rules or deferral to standard law as a substantial source of law or overseeing source in specific settings.

During a crisis, the legitimate position and jobs of key authorities ought to be characterized in law. Laws may approve forces and power to make moves that are sensibly needed to manage a genuine danger to public health, for example, extend the medical services or crisis the executives labour force; hold onto property to build up crisis reaction focuses and to guarantee the accessibility and fast dissemination of meds and supplies; direct observation and order immunizations, treatment, disconnection or isolate of infected or conceivably infected people; and closure of organizations and premises.

The activity of these forces should be founded on public health contemplations and incorporate reasonable remuneration for the individuals who have endured financial misfortune because of a general wellbeing request influencing their property or offices.

3.2 Responses of States towards the COVID-19 Pandemic

States fanatically guard against infringement on their power over general health administration. Studies have demonstrated that while they were steady of WHO's dynamic methodology during the SARS plague, States reasserted sway during the conversation on modifying IHR.[34] Notwithstanding giving a lot of power to WHO to act in public health, member states pronounce in Article 3(4) of IHR that states have, as per the Charter of the United Nations and the standards of international, the sovereign option to administer and to execute enactment in the compatibility of their health approaches.[35]

Public reactions to the pandemic have shifted fundamentally regarding the utilization of crisis powers, public health measures, institutional interruption, social strategies, and government assistance. To illustrate the divergent responses to the COVID-19 pandemic the study will look at how the following select countries dealt with the pandemic focusing of their key policy and legal responses.

3.2.1 United Kingdom Response to COVID-19

In the United Kingdom, the COVID-19 reaction has been driven by the public government; the decayed organizations of Wales, Scotland, and Northern Ireland; the secretary of state for wellbeing; and the central clinical and logical officials—with the National Health Service (NHS) going about as the essential medical services supplier. The United Kingdom's case is educational in 2 habits. The first is the limitation of the controls incorporated into the public

---

[34] Eyal Benvenisti, 'The WHO - Destined to Fail?: Political Cooperation and the COVID-19 Pandemic' [2020] SSRN Electronic Journal.
[35] International Health Regulations (IHR) (Geneva: World Health Organization, 2005), art. 3(4)

authority's logical investigation, and the second is the obscure change between logical information and their change into training. The current UK reaction has been divided and mixed up; they need to create nuanced results at pace necessitates that inventive instruments and methods be sent by multidisciplinary entertainers in an organized way. The way wherein the UK government has embraced general wellbeing methods and practice has not exclusively been profoundly political yet in addition ineffectively coordinated to the prerequisites important to react to a novel, quickly spreading high-outcome microorganism.[36]

3.2.2 United States Response to COVID-19

The United States has reacted to the COVID-19 pandemic at all degrees of government. Congress has authorized the enactment of various legislations and the President and the chief organizations have declared guidelines and guidelines and made another move to execute reactions to COVID-19 to reduce financial and social effects. State governments across the United States have established crisis rules and enactment to react to the COVID-19 pandemic. In certain occurrences, state lead representatives have given different requests announcing highly sensitive situations, approving leader activity. State councils likewise have instituted crisis enactment giving subsidizing to reactions to the pandemic and performing oversight over the certain chief and legal activities. Three instances of activities of state chief position and three instances of activities of state authoritative authority are given beneath.[37]

3.3.3 South Africa Response to COVID-19

South Africa's response to the COVID involved eight critical stages. The first stage was centred around planning for Covid-19, including building up the testing limit. The next stage involved

---

[36] Gemma Bowsher, Rose Bernard and Richard Sullivan, 'A Health Intelligence Framework for Pandemic Response: Lessons from the UK Experience of COVID-19' (2020) 18 Health Security.
[37] The Law Library of Congress, 'United States: Federal, State, and Local Government Responses to COVID-19' (2020).

prohibition on international travel, shut down of schools, limiting get-togethers and advancing social distancing and hand cleanliness. Stage the consisted of a national lockdown while stage four saw the deployment of community health workers to the highest-risk communities to undertake active house-to-house case finding. Stage five included identification of problem areas and usage of counteraction measures in regions with restricted episodes. Stage six is centred around giving clinical consideration, including developing field medical clinics, some in-assembly halls. Stage seven included planning for funerals, entombments, and the psychological wellness challenges related to deprivation. The last stage centred around remaining watchful by participating on the off chance that discovering exercises and observing populace insusceptibility levels utilizing surveys in anticipation of resulting pandemic waves.[38]

3.3 Towards a Global Response to the COVID-19 Pandemic

International law has proven to unfit to relieve the danger of COVID-19, raising a goal for global legitimate changes to explain state commitments, encourage lawful responsibility, and acknowledge global health security. Such comprehensive changes of international law will require either the undertaking of essential corrections to the IHR system or the improvement of another international legal instrument to structure the administration of global health.

As a worldwide lawful structure for worldwide wellbeing security, WHO assumes an organizing part in the worldwide observation and revealing framework made by the IHR, supporting partner states in reinforcing health frameworks and building public health limits. Rather than now meeting up to defy the COVID-19 pandemic through worldwide administration, states have returned to independent strategies, international rivalry, unfair assaults, and worldwide disregard.

---

[38] Salim S Abdool Karim, 'The South African Response to the Pandemic' (2020) 382 The New England Journal of Medicine.

In the battle against COVID-19 pandemic, international law plays a vital role and given that the pandemic is a global issue, it cannot be managed singularly by states. Instead, to viable deal with the pandemic, states should coordinate through international law. Perhaps the inadequacy of international law stems from the major criticism of international law that it is insufficient in tending to global issues due to the non-compliance by states to the rules and lack of effective enforcement mechanisms. This apparent inadequacy could be attributed to the design of the international legal order, which has been structurally organized in accordance with free sovereign States that disregard any form of superior authority.

4.0   CONCLUSION

This study has attempted to provide a comprehensive analysis of the role of international law in the context of the COVID-19 pandemic. The emergence of the COVID-19 pandemic highlights the importance of international law and the role it can play in dealing with a global health crisis. In an attempt to provide analytical backing to this assertion, the research has examined the role of international in the context of the COVID-19 pandemic. Accordingly, the pandemic has brought into the limelight the shortcoming of international law in terms of the lack of an authoritative and adequately enforceable obligation on States to curb pandemics inside their boundaries or to assist different States with containing their pandemics. To conclude, it is observed recommended that while states opt to adopt unilateral nationalistic approaches in dealing with the COVID-19 pandemic, the panacea for our mutual survival as humanity lies in the capacity of an international organization to deal with a global pandemic without a national agenda towards the realisation of the fundamental role of international law.

LIST OF REFERENCES

Abdool Karim SS, 'The South African Response to the Pandemic' (2020) 382 The New England Journal of Medicine

Barry JM, *GREAT INFLUENZA : The Story of the Deadliest Pandemic in History.* (Penguin Books 2020)

Benedictow O, 'The Black Death: The Greatest Catastrophe Ever | History Today' (*Historytoday.com*, 2005) <https://www.historytoday.com/archive/black-death-greatest-catastrophe-ever> accessed 31 December 2020

Benvenisti E, 'The WHO - Destined to Fail?: Political Cooperation and the COVID-19 Pandemic' [2020] SSRN Electronic Journal

Bowsher G, Bernard R and Sullivan R, 'A Health Intelligence Framework for Pandemic Response: Lessons from the UK Experience of COVID-19' (2020) 18 Health Security

Bull H, *The Anarchical Society : A Study of Order in World Politics* (Columbia University Press 2012)

Crawford J, *Brownlie's Principles of Public International Law.* (9th edn, Oxford University Press 2019)

Damir Huremović, *Psychiatry of Pandemics : A Mental Health Response to Infection Outbreak* (Cham Springer International Publishing Imprint,Springer 2019)

DeWitte SN, 'Mortality Risk and Survival in the Aftermath of the Medieval Black Death' (2014) 9 PLoS ONE <https://www.ncbi.nlm.nih.gov/pmc/articles/PMC4013036/>

Flecknoe D, Wakefield BC and Simmons A, 'Plagues & Wars: The "Spanish Flu" Pandemic as a Lesson from History' (2018) 34 Medicine, Conflict and Survival

Gostin LO, 'Global Health Security in an Era of Explosive Pandemic Potential' [2019] SSRN Electronic Journal

Gostin LO, Habibi R and Meier BM, 'Has Global Health Law Risen to Meet the COVID-19 Challenge? Revisiting the International Health Regulations to Prepare for Future Threats' (2020) 48 The Journal of Law, Medicine & Ethics

Gostin LO and Wiley LF, *Public Health Law : Power, Duty, Restraint* (University Of California Press 2016)

'IHR Emergency Committee on Novel Coronavirus (2019-NCoV)' (*www.who.int*) <https://www.who.int/director-general/speeches/detail/who-director-general-s-statement-on-ihr-emergency-committee-on-novel-coronavirus-(2019-ncov)> accessed 31 December 2020

Katz R and Kornblet S, 'Comparative Analysis of National Legislation in Support of the Revised International Health Regulations: Potential Models for Implementation in the United States' (2010) 100 American Journal of Public Health

Patton S, 'The Peace of Westphalia and It Affects on International Relations, Diplomacy and Foreign Policy' (2019) 10 The Histories: <https://digitalcommons.lasalle.edu/the_histories/vol10/iss1/5> accessed 31 December 2020

Phelan A and Gostin LO, 'Farewell to the God of Plague: Has International Law Prepared Us for the next Pandemic?' (2014) 15 Georgetown Journal of International Affairs <https://www.jstor.org/stable/43773636> accessed 31 December 2020

Pons Rafols X, 'International Law and Global Health: An Overview' [2015] Paix et Securite Internationales

Scheidel W, *The Great Leveler : Violence and the History of Inequality from the Stone Age to the Twenty-First Century / Walter Scheidel.* (Princeton University Press 2017)

Snowden FM, *Epidemics and Society : From the Black Death to the Present* (Yale University Press 2019)

'Summary of Probable SARS Cases with Onset of Illness from 1 November 2002 to 31 July 2003' (*www.who.int*) <https://www.who.int/publications/m/item/summary-of-probable-sars-cases-with-onset-of-illness-from-1-november-2002-to-31-july-2003> accessed 31 December 2020

The Law Library of Congress, 'United States: Federal, State, and Local Government Responses to COVID-19' (2020)

Tyrrell DAJ and others, 'Coronaviridae' (1975) 5 Intervirology

WHO, 'Listings of WHO's Response to COVID-19' (*www.who.int*, 2020) <https://www.who.int/news/item/29-06-2020-covidtimeline> accessed 31 December 2020

——, 'WHO Director-General's Opening Remarks at the Media Briefing on COVID-19 - 11 March 2020' (*www.who.int*, 2020) <https://www.who.int/director-general/speeches/detail/who-director-general-s-opening-remarks-at-the-media-briefing-on-covid-19---11-march-2020> accessed 31 December 2020

World Health Organization, *Constitution of the World Health Organization.* (The Organization 1989)

——, *International Health Regulations (2005).* (World Health Organization 2016)

——, 'Naming the Coronavirus Disease (COVID-19) and the Virus That Causes It' (*www.who.int*, 2020) <https://www.who.int/emergencies/diseases/novel-coronavirus-2019/technical-guidance/naming-the-coronavirus-disease-(covid-2019)-and-the-virus-that-causes-it> accessed 31 December 2020

——, 'WHO COVID-19 Dashboard' (*covid19.who.int*, 2020) <https://covid19.who.int/> accessed 31 December 2020